GOAL SETTER TO GOAL GETTER

HOW TO ACHIEVE YOUR GOALS AND NOT JUST SET THEM

SHELLY SHULMAN

authors
AND CO.

CONTENTS

ACKNOWLEDGEMENTS

Writing a book was certainly more challenging than I imagined it would be, but it was an amazing experience.

I'd like to thank

My Family
Daniel, Fiona, Kelsie and Max
Thank you for your patience and support during the writing of this book. I could not have done it without you.

To Team Fish Finger
Victoria and Natalie
Thank you for your endless encouragement, support and bum-kicking when needed.

To Bethany
For being my guinea pig and first reader and giving me the encouraging feedback that gave me the boost I needed.

And finally

You
The person reading this book - thank you for taking the time to read it. I hope you enjoy it.

INTRODUCTION

You're caught in a trap. Stuck in what feels like an eternal rut. Frustrated with the direction your life and business are taking. You have dreams and aspirations you want to achieve but you have no idea where to start and at the minute you just aren't getting the results that you want. The mind monkeys are telling you that goals for personal self-gratification are wrong. You don't want to be called selfish. You are worried you will be judged for putting your wants and needs above, or even just alongside, those of others.

You feel everything you once did seemed to revolve around the routines and needs of others. You were serving them and putting their needs and wants above your own, but now they have moved on and despite working so hard to get them what they wanted, you are still in the same place. You've been everything to everybody and always put yourself last. You know that you have reached that point when it's time for change, but you have absolutely no idea how or where to even start. How do you start to move forward? Where do you start making changes and improvements towards the life you really want?

Change is hard. It's scary to step from the security blanket of that regular routine into the unknown, and you don't feel you have the confidence to take that leap.

But you're tired. That routine that used to bring you so much comfort and structure and joy is now mundane. It served a purpose at one point in time, but times have changed. Things around you have moved forward and there you are, stuck in the same place. You don't want to continue to go through life on autopilot, always doing the same things and always getting the same results. You know you were destined for more.

Unhappy with your current situation, you are taking your frustrations out on your loved ones. Perhaps subconsciously you are envious of them. From the outside they seem to have it all. They are off living their fabulous lives and you have somehow got left behind. And behind that envy, a feeling of resentment is starting to fester. You feel a little angry at the unfairness of it all. You gave your life for their successes and now compared to theirs your life feels a bit of a failure.

But you are scared to 'rock the boat'. You have fallen into a pattern where perhaps it is easier to stay quiet. Perhaps you are worried about being misunderstood; scared of being laughed at; afraid to create conflict and potentially up-end relationships with people who are used to you behaving a certain way. Who are you to follow your dreams and ask for what you want?

Let me tell you! You are an incredible soul who has every right to live the life you desire without apologies.

It is time to leave all those negative feelings in the past, have faith and take strategic action to move forward. Don't wait — jump before you are pushed. Take control of your own destiny.

In the 2008 film *The Women* there is a great part where Bette Midler's character says to Meg Ryan's character, "Don't give a shit about anybody. Be selfish. Because once you ask yourself the question, *'What about me?'* everything changes for the better." This is such an important message to hear. We are so often told that we need to be selfless and put others first.

We need to start understanding that it's not wrong or selfish to put yourself first. On an aeroplane you are instructed to put your own oxygen mask on before you help others. You need to do that to be in a better position to help other people. I apply exactly the same logic to goal setting. My business and I need to be in the best possible shape to be able to do great things for other people too.

The last time someone asked me what I really wanted was when I was a child and I was asked what I wanted for my birthday or Christmas. It's time to get real.

Who are *you?* What do *you* want?

Utilising the skills you already have (and trust me, you have more than you think), combined with the knowledge you will gain from this book, you will be in the position to set goals, make changes, move forward, and live the lifestyle you truly desire.

Over the years I have set goals and moved my life forward many, many times. From being a stay-at-home mum to being a home business owner. From a home business to premises. There has even been a complete business rebrand after nine years.

Most recently I moved from a product-based business to a service-based business. And the majority of these changes occurred after I had been diagnosed with bipolar. Nothing was going to stand in my way of me living my best life and getting what I wanted. Nothing!

Each time I have 'up-levelled' I have come out the other side stronger and more experienced. I've grown so much in confidence that I don't even recognise the person that I once used to be. Every accomplishment, no matter how small, has helped me to believe in myself more.

And more importantly, I am now living the life that is right for me. Not the life that others think I should live. Not a life that leaves me sacrificing my own wants and desires to make others happy. I learned to start putting myself first. And when I started putting myself first, those around me benefitted more.

When you implement the goal-setting skills you will learn in this book, you will go on to experience the freedom and lifestyle you desire. Whether that is turning that hobby into a paying job, getting more free time to spend with your family, or earning more money, you will be living the life *you* want to live and achieving the things *you* want to achieve. You will be happier, more content, and more relaxed.

Being open and honest with those close to you about what you want and need won't damage true relationships. It will make them stronger. They'll have respect for you.

You will take those next steps into your future with confidence and certainty that you are on the right path with the right support.

How do I know this?

I have been exactly where you are right now. I have experienced every emotion that you have felt, such as clinging on for dear life, being afraid to take the leap, and hoping that change will just magically happen overnight. And one day I just let go. I decided that I wanted something more – something better. I went out and got it, and my life is all the better for it.

You will be walking a path that many others, including myself, have walked before you.

Others who decided it was time to set goals and made it happen.

Like K, who had no idea how to market her business when she first started to work with me. She has grown in confidence, improved her money mindset and started charging her worth with ease. She has expanded her business into avenues she only dreamed of before and her business continues to grow.

Or A, who, since setting business goals, is now so much more organised and relaxed that it has changed her lifestyle.

Or like hundreds of people who have elevated in confidence, stretched their comfort zone, and revolutionised their lives, because they decided it was time to ask themselves, "What do I want?" and they took the action that was needed to make it happen.

This book is not a magic wand, nor is it the silver bullet to a dream life, but my promise to you is that if you go on this journey with me, as others have before you, and take action, you will be able to achieve the results you want.

Your life will change in the way *you* want it to.

You will be in control of your own destiny.

I will be showing you that your goals are as individual as your fingerprints. They can be big or small but the process to achieve them is the same.

I will show you how to get results quicker by breaking goals into bite-sized chunks and get you hooked on getting results.

We will dig deep into your why and work out what you want and why you want it and then we'll go through a proven step-by-step method to make it happen.

Most importantly, I'll be showing you that setting and achieving goals is actually fun.

By the end of the book, you'll have gone from goal setter to goal getter.

This is my personal invitation to you to start getting what you want by turning the page and starting on the first step of your new journey. It's time to move forward in a more positive direction.

With gratitude,

Shelly

1

THE IMPORTANCE OF GOAL SETTING

The first step to achieving success as a female entrepreneur is understanding the power of goal setting. This is where I went totally wrong when I first started my business. I never set any goals. Not one. Don't get me wrong, I had dreams and aspirations of the kind of things I wanted to achieve, but never anything concrete. It was all more pie in the sky kind of stuff at that point. More of an "It would be cool if this happened."

So let me start by sharing the information I needed at the beginning: what goal setting actually is.

Put simply, goal setting is a process that helps you to identify what you want to achieve and to create a plan of action to get there. It is one of the most important skills that, as female entrepreneurs, we should possess. It is the process of setting goals and then taking action to achieve them. The key part of that is 'taking action', and I'll cover that later in the book.

When done correctly, goal setting can help you achieve the success you desire, not only in your business but in your life, as a lot of goals that we set ourselves are directly related to what we want our lives to look like. They are all interlinked.

In this first chapter, I will discuss the importance of goal setting, the benefits of setting goals, how goal setting can help achieve business success, achieving goals, and the common goal-setting mistakes to avoid.

So, let's get started.

The importance of goal setting

Setting goals is one of the most important things that as an entrepreneur you do for your business. When you have a goal or goals to work towards, it gives you a clear path to follow and helps you to focus your attention on what you want to achieve. Without goals, and without that sense of direction, your business can, and most probably will, take on a mind of its own and will grow in a direction you don't want to be going in.

It is what happened to me with my first business. The business grew and grew which was great. Or so I thought. But ultimately, I ended up with too many orders, overwhelmed, burned out and having a mental breakdown sitting on the floor of my kitchen. Not so great. And it's not something I would wish on anyone, even my worst enemy.

When you have clear goals, it is easier to take all the necessary actions and steps to reach the targets you have set for yourself. Without them, it can be easy to lose sight of what you're trying to achieve and get side-tracked and not make the progress you want in your business. And that's where it's easy to get disheartened and want to quit.

Having goals allows you to measure your progress and see how far you've come. This can be a huge motivator, especially when you're feeling stuck or like you're not making any progress, because you have usually made more progress than you think you have. Just because you haven't reached the 'end' goal, doesn't mean you haven't moved forward. And seeing just how far you've come can give you the boost you need to keep going. On the flip side, if you aren't progressing as quickly as you anticipated, it also allows you to see what isn't working, so you can make changes if needed and you aren't flogging a dead horse, as it were.

Having goals can also help to keep you accountable, and when you have someone to hold you accountable, it can be a lot easier to stay on track and achieve your goals. Statistically, you are 95% more likely to achieve your goals if you tell someone what they are and ask them to hold you accountable. **95%**

Compare that to the following probabilities of achieving your goals….

- Having an idea or goal: 10% likely to complete the goal
- Consciously deciding that you will do it: 25%
- Deciding when you will do it: 40%
- Planning how to do it: 50%
- Committing to someone that you will do it: 65%
- Having a specific accountability appointment with someone you've committed to: 95%

The value of having someone to help you achieve your goals and keep you accountable is clear. Having accountability also helps to push you outside of your comfort zone and forces you to act. Also, it's when we step out of our comfort zone that all the fun stuff happens.

All these reasons highlight why you need to put such a high emphasis on setting goals, not just for your business, but also for your life. It is so important for you to have clear goals that you are working towards. Without goals, it can be very difficult to make the progress and achieve the success you want in your business and your life.

The benefits of setting goals

When it comes to goal setting the benefits are endless, but let's look at a few of the key benefits that you can experience. And let's be honest, we all do love the benefits of anything we do.

The most obvious benefit is that goal setting will help you to grow your business. For most entrepreneurs this is our biggest fundamental goal. We want to grow a successful, profitable business so we can live the lifestyle we want to live. When we have specific goals in mind, and we know the reasons why we have set those goals, we can focus our efforts on achieving them. And when we achieve those goals, and we can see the tangible results of our hard work, this can be extremely motivating and can lead to even more success down the road. It's a snowball effect!

Another benefit to goal setting is that it is helping you to stay focused on what is important. We can put the blinkers on, get our heads down and do what we need to do. We can get rid of the shiny object syndrome and focus on what is essential to getting the results we want. When you have a clear goal in mind, it is easier to say "no" to distractions and side projects. (Yes, you have to get used to saying no but I promise it starts to get really easy.) This allows you to put all your energy into achieving your main goal, which will lead to better results.

Setting goals also gives you a sense of direction. Think of it like a sat nav. Your goal is your end destination. You plot a 'route' to achieve that goal and then you follow it. This can be especially helpful when you are first starting out as an entrepreneur and are still finding your feet. Having specific goals to aim for can help you to stay on track and avoid veering off in the wrong direction. No one wants to end up in the 'wrong end of town'.

Increasing your chances of success is another benefit to setting goals. Studies have shown that people who set goals are more likely to achieve success than those who do not. This is because setting a goal gives you something to work towards and makes it more likely that you will take the necessary steps to achieve it.

And, last but not least, goal setting can help you live the life you want to live. This is because when you have specific goals, you are able to create a roadmap for your life. You can map out exactly where you want to go and what you need to do in order to get there and live the life you want, whatever that looks like for you. This can help you avoid making decisions that could potentially derail your journey.

How goal setting can help you achieve success

Goal setting and task performance were studied by Locke and Latham (1991). Goal setting theory is based upon the simplest of introspective observations, specifically, that conscious human behaviour is purposeful. Since people often behave in ways that are inconsistent with their conscious intentions, much research has been devoted to understanding what factors influence goal-directed behaviour.

A great deal of this research has focused on the role of motivation in task performance. Theories of motivation generally fall into one of two camps: those that emphasise intrinsic factors and those that emphasise extrinsic factors. Intrinsic motivation occurs when people are driven to perform a task because they find it personally rewarding. Extrinsic motivation, on the other hand, arises from external factors such as rewards or punishments.

Intrinsic and extrinsic motivation play a role in achieving goals and getting results. When you have a clear understanding of your own personal motivation, you can set goals that reflect your true desires. This will help ensure that you stay on track and achieve success.

Both intrinsic and extrinsic motivation are important for achieving goals. Intrinsic motivation is necessary for sustaining interest in a task, while extrinsic motivation can provide the initial push needed to get started.

It is important to find a balance between intrinsic and extrinsic motivation in order to achieve long-term success. Over-reliance on either one can lead to burnout or apathy.

I myself have always had a mix of both intrinsic and extrinsic motivation. I love the satisfaction of a job well done but I always love a reward too. It's about finding that balance.

For example, when my goal was to quit alcohol, of course, intrinsically I had a massive sense of satisfaction, but I also rewarded myself with treats along the way, such as a new Mulberry bag when I hit my first 'mini' goal of thirty days sober.

However, when it comes to business goals, as much as personally performing a task because I find it rewarding is great, it is important not to fall into the trap of doing everything yourself. Learning to delegate and outsource is key.

You will know personally what works best for you and you may find that you need different types of motivation for different goals.

Achieving your goals

We will go into this in more detail as the book goes on but achieving your goals really does give you the biggest sense of satisfaction. The psychological factor of this is that winning creates dopamine. Dopamine is known as the feel-good hormone. The presence of dopamine in the brain creates feelings of happiness, euphoria and pleasure. In other words, it feels good to win. You get hooked on that success so you want to do it again. In turn that creates more sustained motivation.

It is also important to celebrate each success along the way. It is positive reinforcement, which I know is a phrase normally used when raising children and training dogs but hear me out. You can use a simple system of rewards to keep yourself motivated.

For every day that you stick to taking action, give yourself a small treat. It can be something as simple as watching an extra half hour of television or taking a longer break between writing sessions. This positive reinforcement will help you maintain your focus and dedication to reaching your goals.

One of the main reasons that entrepreneurs give up on their goals is because they get discouraged when they don't see results immediately. It's important to keep in mind that Rome wasn't built in a day, and neither will your successful business be. Goal setting is a marathon, not a sprint. No one decides to enter the London Marathon and runs twenty-six miles on the first day of training! Trust the process and have faith in yourself and your ability to reach your goals.

Goal setting really is one of the most important aspects of any business, and it's especially important for female entrepreneurs who are often juggling a lot of responsibilities. We wear so many hats and are spinning so many plates. If we're not careful, it's easy to get pulled in a million different directions and lose focus on what's really important. That's why setting goals is so important.

2

HOW TO SET EFFECTIVE GOALS

I t is not enough to just set goals, you have to set *effective* goals if you want to achieve them. Why is it important to set effective goals? Because if your goals are not effective, you will not achieve them. And if you don't achieve your goals, what's the point of setting them in the first place? No one likes wasting their time.

The first year I finally started to set goals, I didn't achieve a lot of them, because they weren't good goals for me at that point in my life and my business. I was still figuring things out and my goals were all over the place. They were goals that other people had told me that I should be setting. They were goals that I saw other people setting and thought, 'If that's what they are doing, that's what I need to be doing.' They weren't aligned with what I wanted to achieve.

If you want to set effective goals that you *will* achieve, there are a few things you need to know. In this chapter, we will discuss how to brainstorm and set effective goals as well as the importance of goal alignment.

We will also look at the different types of goals and how to create a plan to achieve them.

Brainstorming goals and setting goals that you are in alignment with

When it comes to goal setting, you first need to brainstorm what you want to achieve. This could be anything from specific, tangible goals, such as earning a certain amount of money within a certain timeframe or wanting to write and publish a book, to loftier aims such as wanting to get an OBE. (Yes, an OBE is one of my long-term goals. Reach for the moon and you'll hit the stars and all that.) However, it's important that you set goals that you are in alignment with. This means that the goals fit with your core values and what you want to achieve in life, not what other people think you should be doing.

It can be helpful to sit down with a pen and paper, or even just use the notes function on your phone and brainstorm a list of potential goals. At this initial point, don't limit yourself by what you think is achievable. The sky's the limit! When I started writing my goals, I took myself back to being a kid at Christmas and writing a list for Santa, back to those days when we all knew exactly what it was we wanted. We didn't think about any limitations. (Thich is why I always asked for a pony without any thought as to where we would keep it.) And that's what you should do when brainstorming goals.

If you have ever watched the 2008 film *The Women* with Meg Ryan, there is a great part of the film where she takes a piece of paper and writes in the middle, *What do I want?* She then starts to 'scrapbook' around it. This is what you should do. Write in the middle of a piece of paper or on your notes app,

What do I want? Start brainstorming all of the things that you want.

Some people like to set goals in different areas of their life, such as health and fitness, personal development, business, finance, relationships, etc. But at this point I prefer to just write down everything that I want, regardless of where it fits in my life.

Once you have a list of potential goals, it's time to start narrowing them down.

The first step is to look at whether the goals are in alignment with what you want to achieve. This means that the goals fit with your core values, otherwise you will never be truly satisfied with what you achieve. For example, if one of your core values is freedom, then a goal that requires you to work long hours in an office is not in alignment with what you want to achieve. On the other hand, a goal that gives you the freedom to work from home or pursue your passion is in alignment with your core value of freedom.

It is important to take some time to consider what is truly important to you, as this will help you to set goals that are both exciting and achievable. If you're not excited about a goal, then it's likely that you won't be committed to achieving it. Your goals need to light you up inside. Likewise, if a goal feels too out of reach, then it can also be demotivating. Therefore, finding the right balance between excitement and achievability is key.

When I first set goals, I wrote down *a new car*. That goal stayed on my goals list for three years because it didn't light me up inside. I wasn't all that bothered about it, and I only achieved the goal because someone drove into my car (on my birthday, might I add) and wrote it off. I achieved my goal by default.

How to set effective goals

There are a few key things to keep in mind when it comes to set effective goals.

Your goals need to have a purpose. They should be something that you are excited about and that fit with your core values. For example, your overall purpose may be to empower other women, but a goal to achieve that might be to start a blog and write about your experiences as a woman in today's society. Another goal may be to become a mentor for young women starting out in their careers. By having purposeful goals, we can ensure that we are moving closer towards the life we want to live. You will also be driven by the desire to make a difference in the world.

Your goals need to be intuitive. They must be something you want to do, not something you think you should be doing. When I first set goals, a lot of the things on my list were goals I thought I 'should' be setting because it's what other people in my circle had on their goals list. But the truth is, I didn't really want to do any of those things. So, my goals either remained unfulfilled and I felt terrible about myself because of it, or I did fulfil them but I didn't get a great sense of satisfaction.

Case in point. A pair of Christian Louboutin shoes. I had these on my list. I had to have the red soles and I dutifully achieved my goal. But I have worn them once. Realistically, I knew they were uncomfortable when I bought them. But I was in denial, and I 'had' to buy them because I had to tick off my goal. (Give me a pair of New Look wide fit any day!)

I ended up selling said pair of shoes and I sat down and thought about what *I* really wanted to achieve. It was at that point my goals started to feel more attainable and exciting. And more me!

Your goals need to be something you are committed to achieving. If you aren't committed to doing the work to make the goal a reality, then it won't happen. It's that simple. It would be like me setting myself a goal to run a marathon. I would never be committed to doing all the training. I know I wouldn't. If you really aren't feeling it, don't put it down. It will be that task on the to do list that gets moved over week after week but never actually gets done.

You also need to make sure you keep the SMART framework in mind:

Specific: Make sure your goals are specific. When I ask my clients what they want to achieve, I don't want vague answers. I don't just want to hear them say they want to go on holiday. That's not a specific goal. I want to hear them say, "I want to go to Dubai for two weeks in August. I want to go and stay in this hotel and it's going to cost me this amount." That's a specific goal.

By the same principle, wanting to make more money is not a specific goal. You need to be able to give values. How much money do you want to make? It's ok to have an actual figure to write down. Earning and talking about money is not a bad thing. We need to change that!

Measurable: This means that your goal needs to be something that you can keep track of. Weight loss is always a good example of this. You know how much overall weight you want to lose, and you keep track of your progress each week. Financial targets are also a good one and probably the most obvious but social media goals can also be measurable. You can set yourself a goal to increase your engagement by a certain amount. Or to grow a Facebook group to a certain number of people. You don't want a vague never-ending goal or a goal you can tick off once you've done a tiny amount. "I want to earn more money" is too vague a goal. Technically you can tick that off when you've earned an extra 10p and that kind of defeats the object.

Attainable: Your goal should be attainable – not unrealistic. If it's your first year in business, setting a goal of turning over £1 million in the next twelve months is probably not all that realistic. Make sure your goal is reasonable considering your current situation. Don't be signing yourself up for a marathon next month if you haven't been running for years. Start with Couch to 5k. There is no reason why that £1 million goal won't come in the future if your goals are smart and achievable at the beginning. Set it as your long-term goal instead (we'll talk about those later).

Relevant: Make sure that your goals align with you and with your bigger picture. Your goals should always contribute to your bigger goals. For example, a goal of wanting to make £2,500 in sales in a week is relevant if your overall goal is to make six figures in a year. Learning how to do Facebook Ads is relevant if you want to increase your visibility.

Time-bound: Your goals need to have a defined start and end date. It's ok to set a goal at the start of the year but plan to start in May. No one expects you to tackle all your goals immediately at one go. But it is important you have an end date. And don't be a deadline dancer either. Don't put a goal off because you still have another two months to go. Your goal will be a lot easier if you break it down into eight weekly chunks rather than trying to get it all done in a week!

As an example, here is how to make a broad goal into a smart goal. A broad goal example would be 'I want to write a book'. The smart version would be:

- Specific: I will write a book about social media that is a minimum of 150 pages long.
- Measurable: I will write one chapter per month or three to five pages per week.
- Attainable: I have years of experience of helping businesses enhance their social media. I can self-publish a book easily on Amazon.
- Relevant: Writing a book about social media will help me establish myself as an expert and go towards my business visibility and growth.
- Time-bound: My book will be completed and ready to be published in ten months.

What are the different types of goals?

There are lots of different types of goals but the three main goals most entrepreneurs set themselves are business goals, personal goals and learning goals. It's important to have a variety of different goals and a mix of all three.

Business goals are specific objectives that you want your business to achieve. They could include increasing sales, audience growth, expanding into new markets or adding new products or services.

Personal goals are specific to you as an individual rather than your business. They could include things like developing new skills, improving your work-life balance, or taking on a new challenge.

Learning goals are all about acquiring new knowledge and understanding. They could involve learning more about your industry, keeping up to date with changes in technology or studying for a professional qualification.

Sometimes goals may encompass all three areas. In 2020, during lockdown, I decided to take the time to study an online course with Yale University on the Science of Well Being. It started as a personal goal, as something to do to prevent boredom. But it became a learning goal and also benefitted my business as I was able to implement what I learned and pass that knowledge on to my clients.

Why is it important to have a mix of different types of goals?

Having a mix of different types of goals is important because it helps to keep you motivated and focused. If all your goals are business-related, for example, you might find it easy to become discouraged if you don't see results immediately. Having personal and learning goals as well will help to keep you motivated and give you a sense of achievement even when your business goals aren't being met.

It is also important to have a mix of long-term and short-term goals. Long-term goals are the big objectives you want to achieve over the next year or two (or five), while short-term goals are the smaller steps you'll take to get there. Having both will help you to stay focused and keep moving forward even when you encounter setbacks.

Mapping out a plan to achieve your goals

It is important to have a plan in place to achieve your goals. This means that you need to know what you need to do in order to accomplish them. You also need to set a deadline for yourself and make sure that your goals are realistic. It's important to be motivated and push yourself, but you don't want to set yourself up for failure by setting goals that are too high.

One way to make sure that you have a plan in place is to break your goals down into smaller, more manageable pieces. This will make them seem less daunting and more achievable. You can also create a timeline for yourself so that you can see your progress and stay on track.

For example – a goal could be to get an extra 3000 email subscribers over a twelve-month period. That becomes 250 a month, which becomes 62.50 a week. When planning out each week in my business, I ask myself what I am doing to reach that target. Where am I posting about my lead magnet? What am I doing to collect email addresses? I set tasks for the week that are related to those questions. At the end of the week, I review the numbers. If it works great, I do the same thing the following week. If it doesn't, I make changes.

Breaking it down into smaller chunks takes away that sense of overwhelm. The bigger goal can seem overwhelming. The weekly goals are more manageable. A yearly goal of an extra £12,000 becomes £1000 a month, which then comes down to just an extra £250 a week. Smaller chunks are what makes those bigger goals more manageable and easier to track.

And what gets measured gets managed.

It is also important to remember that your goals can change over time. As you accomplish certain goals, you may find that you want to set new ones. That's perfectly normal. Just make sure that you adjust your plan accordingly so that you can continue making progress.

3

THE POWER OF VISUALISATION

I will be honest. I was hesitant about including a chapter about visualisation. After all, how can something as intangible as a feeling or image have any impact on our lives? But I also know that it is a tool that many use to help achieve their goals and desires, so it seemed wrong to exclude it.

I should clarify at this point that I don't believe in the whole asking the universe and it shall appear... *thing*. I've been asking the universe to deliver me Gary Barlow for years and I am still waiting. I do, however, think that if we have a clear idea of what it is we want to achieve, and we focus on that regularly, then it is more likely to happen.

A great example of this in action is a recent affiliate launch I took part in. I told my affiliate manager that morning I wanted to get fifteen sales by the end of play. During the day I messaged her to say, "Sale number thirteen in the bag," with only two more to go. Less than an hour later she messaged me to say, "You are on fifteen now." Two people had emailed her requesting to be allocated to my sales and get my bonuses. So, I joked, "Sending it out to the universe that I want twenty." I ended on twenty-one. Did the universe get me twenty-one? No. But because it was the number I was visualising and focusing on, I was more conscious of taking the action to make it happen.

Think about it like this: if you want to buy a new car, you are more likely to see one that you like if you are looking for it. If you have a clear image in your mind of the make, model and colour that you want, then you are more likely to spot it when it's for sale. The same goes for other goals and desires. Your subconscious is actively looking for it and you are more likely to take the action needed to get it.

Some people say that visualisation is key to achieving your goals. They believe that if you can see your desired outcome in your mind, it's a sign that you're on the right track.

This chapter is about the power of visualisation for female entrepreneurs in setting and achieving goals. It covers the importance of visualisation in setting and achieving goals, how to create a vision board for your business goals, the power of positive visualisation in manifesting your goals and tips for incorporating visualisation into your goal setting process.

The importance of visualisation in setting and achieving goals

Visualisation is a powerful tool that can be used to achieve goals. By visualising yourself hitting a goal, you're actually training your brain to perform in a way that will help you reach that goal. When you visualise yourself hitting a specific goal, your brain interprets that imagery as reality and creates new neural pathways to support that reality. They say the brain can't tell the difference between the real and the imagined. So, if you can imagine yourself hitting your goal, your brain will start to believe it's possible and take the steps necessary to make it happen.

I remember watching *Wife Swap USA* many years ago and one episode had a couple who were heavily into visualisation. They would spend their weekends doing things like going to open houses for the type of house they wanted to live in and visualising themselves living there. It was all about making their dreams a reality through visualisation. I have to say, I don't really believe in this 'method' of visualisation, and I think that time could have been better spent actually doing work that would allow them to earn the money to live in that house. I would love to know if they ended up getting the house of their dreams in the end.

I am more of a vision board type of person. I take a piece of paper and in the middle I write *What do I want?* and then all around it I write my goals. Some people are more picture based and put pictures of what they want on it. For example, if they want to travel more, they'll put up pictures of different places they'd like to visit. If they want to buy a new car, they'll put up a picture of the make and model they want. I find that vision boards are a great way to keep your goals in front of you so you can see them every day and stay motivated to achieve them. I have mine on the inside of the cupboard door where I keep the tea bags so I see it every morning and it reminds me what I am working for.

How to create a vision board for your business goals

If you're looking for inspiration, take a look at some of the best vision boards on Pinterest. Not only do these boards help you to focus on your goals, but they can also be a lot of fun to make. Just don't get so caught up in making a vision board that you don't take action to make them happen.

To create your own vision board:

1. Start by finding some images or words that represent what you want to achieve. These can be things like pictures of your dream home, or phrases that describe how you want to feel.
2. Once you have a few images or words, start putting them together on a board or piece of paper.
3. Hang your vision board in a place where you'll see it often, such as your office or bedroom (or inside your cupboard where you keep the tea bags).
4. Take a few minutes each day to look at your board and imagine yourself achieving your goals.

Creating a vision board is a great way to focus on your goals and get inspired to achieve them but it's not an excuse not to take action. For some, it's an easy out. An 'I'll put it on the vision board for the future'. But if you want to achieve it in the future the time to take action is now! Don't put it on the vision board and forget about it.

Tips for incorporating visualisation into your goal-setting process

Utilising visualisation as part of your goal-setting process can be very beneficial. There are a few things to keep in mind, however, in order to make sure you're getting the most out of it.

Here are four tips:

1. Make sure your goal is clear and specific. When you're visualising, you want to be able to see yourself achieving your goal in as much detail as possible. This means that it needs to be well defined and easy to imagine.
2. Use positive images and emotions. The better you feel when visualising your goal, the more likely you are to achieve it. Make sure to focus on the positive aspects of achieving your goal and imagine yourself feeling happy and satisfied once you've achieved it.
3. Visualise regularly. The more often you picture yourself achieving your goal, the more likely you are to do so. Try to devote a few minutes each day to visualising yourself succeeding.
4. Stay motivated. It can be easy to get discouraged if you don't see immediate results from visualisation. Remember that it takes time and effort to achieve goals and be sure to stay motivated by focusing on the benefits of achieving your goal.

And above all, don't forget to take *action!* Visualisation is a powerful tool, but it's only one part of the goal-setting process.

You need to take action and work towards your goals in order to achieve them.

4

THE POWER OF TAKING ACTION

When it comes to setting and achieving goals, taking action is essential. Without action, your goals are nothing more than mere words on a piece of paper. It's easy to get caught in the trap of planning and thinking about your goals instead of taking action towards them. Some people actually use planning as a form of procrastination. They think that by planning everything out to the *nth* degree, they'll somehow get it all done perfectly without having to do any real work. But by spending time obsessing over every little detail, they're actually just avoiding taking action.

Interestingly, this behaviour often stems from fear. Fear of failure, fear of the unknown, or even just fear of not being perfect. But here's the thing: no one is perfect. And nothing is ever guaranteed to work out perfectly.

Whilst we touched on visualisation in the last chapter, results only happen when action is taken. Therefore, understanding the power of taking action is key to achieving your goals. This means that you cannot simply sit idly by and expect your goals to be achieved without any effort on your part. You have to do the work. If you aren't taking action you have to ask, are you really committed to achieving your goals? The simple truth is that dreams, visions and goals are achieved and accomplished only through action. As the saying goes, you can't just talk the talk, you have to walk the walk too.

In this chapter, you will learn about the benefits of taking action, how to get started and the importance of taking action towards your goals.

The importance of taking action towards your goals

If you want to achieve your goals, you need to act. It's not enough to just think about them or talk about them; you need to take concrete steps towards making them a reality. This may mean setting a deadline for yourself and working towards it or breaking down your goal into smaller steps that you can work on gradually.

The more you do something, the easier it is to keep going. You can't succeed if your plan doesn't involve any action from start to finish! By maintaining a consistent approach and following through with what's important in this moment – even when times get tough or locations change drastically – you'll find yourself hitting goals faster than ever before without getting overwhelmed by all of these little details that could distract you away from your true intentions.

The key is to make sure that your actions are aligned with your goals. You need to be deliberate about what you're doing and why you're doing it. Every action you take should be moving you closer to your goal. If it's not, then it's a waste of time and energy.

You also need to take action even when you don't feel like it. There will be times when you're tired or unmotivated, but if you push through and do what needs to be done, you'll get closer to your goal.

How to get started taking action towards your goals

So how can you start taking action towards your goals? Here are a few tips:

1. Make a plan: Having a clear plan of what you need to do will help you stay on track. Knowing what you need to do and when you need to do it will help you stay focused and achieve your goals. So, take the time to develop a plan that works for you, and stick to it!

2. Set a deadline: Having a timeline for your goal will help you stay focused and having a specific date to aim for will help you stay on track and achieve success. A deadline gives your goal a sense of urgency and keeps you motivated to achieve it. Remember that you can always adjust your timeline *if* you need to, for example, if you have underestimated how long things may take – *not* if you just aren't showing up to do the work.

3. Break it down into smaller steps: Don't try to do everything at once; break your goal down into smaller, manageable steps. Trying to do too much at once can be overwhelming and lead to discouragement. By setting small, achievable goals, you can stay motivated and see the progress you're making.

4. Take one step at a time: I keep saying it, but Rome wasn't built in a day, and neither are most goals. Breaking down what you need to do into manageable steps will help you move closer to your goal without feeling overwhelmed.

5. Be patient: Progress takes time so don't get discouraged if you don't see results immediately. Trust that the actions you're taking will eventually lead you to your goal.

6. Persevere: There will inevitably be setbacks along the way. However, these challenges and setbacks can actually help us grow and become stronger. So instead of seeing them as roadblocks, let's view them as opportunities for growth. Don't let them stop you from moving forward towards your goal.

Taking action towards your goals can seem daunting, but by following these tips, you can make it happen. Just remember to be patient, stay motivated, and never give up.

The benefits of taking action towards your goals

The benefits of taking actions towards your goals are endless. I remember when I first started setting goals and taking action. It was so satisfying. There was this huge sense of relief that I was doing something constructive that was actually going to get me towards the life I wanted, rather than just being busy for the sake of being busy. Also, the sense of progress was so motivating. Every time I took a step closer to my goal, it made me want to take more action and get even closer. I am quite a competitive person. Others may say very competitive, and it goes back to the message of Chapter One regarding being intrinsically and extrinsically motivated. Once I start something, I am like a dog with a bone until I finish it. And nothing can beat the satisfaction of achieving your goal. There really is no greater feeling.

The benefits of taking action don't stop there. In addition to the great sense of relief and progress, taking action also helps to increase your confidence. The more you do, the more confidence you will have in your ability to achieve your goals. And as your confidence grows, so does your motivation. Suddenly, taking action towards your goals doesn't seem so daunting anymore. In fact, it becomes quite exciting because you know that you are capable of achieving anything you set your mind to.

Back in school days, all my school reports touched on the same thing. *Great worker but lacks confidence.* (Which is ironic, really, seeing as one of my teachers told my parents at parents' evening that I wouldn't amount to much.) Even though I was a typical A grade student, I lacked any confidence in my own abilities. Even when I started running my first business, despite having lots of orders every week, I would spend Mondays on edge, petrified that the clients from the weekend would complain.

You would never think it if you saw me now. People say I'm such a confident person but that is because setting goals and achieving them has made me more confident. It has given me the proof I needed to show myself that I am capable.

Ultimately, the biggest benefit is that when you take action towards your goals, you are more likely to achieve them. It shows that you are committed and determined to get results. Taking action creates a sense of urgency and purpose that drives you to keep going until you reach your destination. It is a bit like a tube of Pringles. Once you've popped you can't stop. Once you start taking action, you won't be able to stop until you achieve your goal. If you find yourself wanting to quit, go back and remind yourself why you set that goal in the first place.

The difference between taking action and not taking action

The consequences of not taking action towards your goals can be disastrous. But if you do take action, you can achieve anything you set your mind to.

Without action you may find yourself in the same spot years down the road, wondering why you haven't made any progress. Worse yet, you may have already given up on your dreams and settled for a life you don't want. You deserve to be happy. You deserve to live a life that fills you with joy. That's where action gets you. I can honestly say now, hand on heart, I am much happier and content than I have ever been. Yes, I still live with bipolar, but my moods are much more stable because I took action. I set out to achieve the life that I wanted to lead.

And that's exactly what you can do too. It doesn't matter where you're starting from. It doesn't matter what your circumstances are. You can make a change for the better, but only if you take action.

We all know that one person who is never happy. The person who moans about everything. Jeez, they would probably even moan about winning the lottery. And usually, these people are never happy because they don't have goals and they never take any constructive action towards changing any of the things they are unhappy with. They just sit around and wait for something to happen. If you're not moving forwards, you're moving backwards. So, ask yourself: are you taking action or inaction?

There are different types of actions you can take to achieve your goals, and it's important to find the right mix that works for you. Some people prefer to take small, consistent actions every day, while others like to take big, bold actions that make a bigger impact. There is no right or wrong way to do things, as long as you're taking action towards your goals.

And if you don't take action towards your goals, here are some of the things you could miss out on:

- Achieving your dreams and reaching your full potential
- Being happy and fulfilled
- Making a difference in the world
- Having a positive impact on those around you

Don't let these opportunities pass you by. Don't wait for something to happen. Make it happen. The power is in your hands.

It is time to get out of your comfort zone and do something that may be difficult. But it's worth it, because taking action is the only way to turn your dreams into reality.

5

HOW TO STAY MOTIVATED AND ACCOUNTABLE

One of the main challenges that entrepreneurs face is staying motivated and accountable to their goals. It's easy to get bogged down in the day-to-day grind and lose sight of your goals. It's even harder to stay motivated when the people around you don't get it. Perhaps they don't run their own business, or they just don't understand your goals.

I remember saying to one of my friends that one goal of mine was to buy a Mulberry handbag. They just scoffed and said, "What's the point? A bag is a bag. It still holds your purse and get fills of receipts." I was so deflated. I had to really sit down and think about what it was that I wanted to achieve and why it mattered to me. And it was at that point I had a lightbulb moment.

It didn't matter what they thought about my goal. It was *my* goal. And I was the only one who could make it happen.

And I've continued to encounter disapproval from some others about my goals and achievements. My Gucci belt— too expensive. My Christian Louboutin make up and pricey moisturiser – too indulgent. Even writing this book raised eyebrows and I was told I'm just doing it to inflate my ego. And every time, rather than getting deflated, I just remember that it's *my* goal and I'm the one who matters. And I continue on my path!

So, how do you stay motivated and accountable to your goals when the people around you just don't get it and everyone around you seems to think you're insane?

Setting up a support system

The first step is to set up a support system of people who *do* get it. These are people who will understand your goals and be supportive of you achieving them. Find a group of like-minded individuals, whether that's online or in person. There are loads of entrepreneur groups out there where you can connect with other business owners. Or you can join an online forum or community related to your industry.

Having a group of supportive people around you will make all the difference when it comes to staying motivated and account-able to your goals. These people will understand what you're going through and be there to help you achieve your goals.

I get that it may seem weird at first that these people may not be your friends and family. They start off as complete strangers, but they will become friends. And they will become an invalu-able part of your support system.

I couldn't survive without mine. I have one long-time friend whom I can talk business with, who is always extremely supportive of my business and goals. My Dad, bless his heart, is extremely proud and very supportive, but doesn't really 'get' what I do for a job (he thinks I play on Facebook all day) so he just asks me on a regular basis if I'm paying my taxes. The rest of my support system are people I have met online. Some of them I haven't even met in real life, but we cheer each other on, give each other advice and support, and it honestly feels like we've been friends for years.

The people in your support system don't necessarily have to be entrepreneurs themselves, but they should at least understand what you're trying to achieve and be supportive of that. And that's sometimes why close friends and family aren't always the best support system as they don't completely understand your life.

It is a bit like crab mentality. You know, when you put crabs in a bucket and one crab tries to escape and the others pull it back down. Your friends and family may not be intentionally dragging you down, but if they don't understand your goals, they might not be as supportive as you need them to be. In their heads they are trying to 'protect' you and keep you safe.

So, find your tribe. Find your people. These are the people who will help you stay motivated and accountable to your goals. And they will make all the difference in helping you achieve success.

Holding yourself accountable

It can be tricky to hold yourself accountable when achieving your goals. You may find yourself making excuses or justifying why you didn't complete a task. Maybe you feel like you don't have enough time, or you're not sure how to get started. Whatever the reason, holding yourself accountable is essential to keeping your motivation high and achieving your goals.

One way to stay accountable is to create a task list and set deadlines for yourself. This will help you stay on track and make sure you are making progress towards your goals. I had deadlines when I was writing this book. I gave myself a deadline to write each chapter and I said to myself that once I had written that chapter I could go and sit in the garden for an hour/watch the next episode of drag race/have a hot tub. I wasn't allowed to do it until after the chapter was done. And it worked.

Plus, there is nothing as satisfying as ticking a task off a to do list.

According to a study on New Year's resolutions, people who achieve their goals often use a technique called stimulus control, by which they frequently remind themselves of those goals. This could involve setting regular reminders on your phone, writing your goals down in a notebook or keeping them visible on a noticeboard.

Seeing your goals written down will help to keep them at the forefront of your mind and make it more likely that you will take action towards achieving them. It's why I have my vision board in my kitchen cupboard. Every time I make a cup of tea, I am reminded of what I am working towards.

You can also post about your goals on social media. When I did a forty-day hula hoop challenge, I posted about it on my Instagram stories and every day I would post a story or a video of me doing my hula hoop. People started to show interest, messaging me to ask how I was getting on. And then, even on the days I really couldn't be bothered, I knew that I still had to show up as people were expecting me. I completed the challenge and it felt great.

Staying motivated to achieve your goals

Motivation comes from many different places. It might be a personal desire to improve yourself or your situation, or to want to set an example for others. Whatever the source of your motivation, focusing on it can help you stay motivated throughout the process of achieving your goals.

When it comes to staying motivated, there are a few key things to keep in mind. One is that it's important to set realistic goals. You're more likely to achieve your goals if you have a plan and are willing to put in the work necessary to reach them. If you know they are too far out of reach you won't even start.

Another helpful tip is to break your goals down into smaller, more manageable pieces. When you have a big goal that seems impossible, it can be demotivating. However, if you break it down into smaller steps, you'll be able to see your progress and feel good about the accomplishments along the way.

Write those accomplishments down as soon as you achieve them. I started to do this because when I looked back to review the year, I could never remember all the fantastic things that I had done. And so, with that in mind, I purposely created a planner with a monthly review section which had space to record what I had achieved each month. When I was having a bad day, which with bipolar is sometimes inevitable, I could look back on what I had achieved. It was written down for me to see in black and white. When your mind is in a down place it can be hard to recall the positive things. That visual reminder was a great motivational boost.

Finally, don't forget to celebrate your successes! If you are extrinsically motivated, treat yourself. When I decided to quit alcohol and I reached thirty days alcohol free, I treated myself to a Mulberry bag. Not every milestone celebration between thirty days and a year was quite as big (my husband was relieved about that) but I celebrated every one in some way, whether it was with a meal out or a trip to the cinema. To be able to say, "I'm doing this today because I achieved xxxx," is extremely rewarding.

When you achieve something big or small, give yourself a moment to relish in it. You did that!

Remember that motivation comes and goes. There will be times when you feel incredibly motivated and inspired, and other times when it's hard to get yourself moving. The key is to keep going even when you're not feeling it. The more you do this, the easier it will become. And eventually, it will become a habit.

Using accountability and motivation to achieve success

It is no secret that accountability and motivation are key to achieving success. Without accountability, it's all too easy to make excuses and give up on your goals. And without motivation, it can be tough to find the drive to keep going. But when you combine the two, you create a powerful force that can help you reach your potential.

When accountability and motivation work together, they create a dynamic duo that can help you achieve anything you set your mind to.

By implementing the tips shared in this chapter, you'll be well on your way to setting and achieving your goals. And remember, if you need help along the way, don't hesitate to ask for it. There's no shame in admitting that you need assistance. In fact, it shows that you're serious about reaching your goals.

6

OVERCOMING OBSTACLES TO GOAL ACHIEVEMENT

I t is one thing to set goals, it's another thing entirely to achieve them. Unfortunately, many people never even get close to their goals because they are stopped in their tracks by obstacles. But these obstacles don't have to stop you. You can overcome them and continue on your path to success. In this chapter, I'll show you how to identify and overcome the most common obstacles to goal achievement so that you can finally reach your full potential.

Identifying obstacles that could stop you achieving your goals

It may seem a strange place to start, looking at reasons why you wouldn't achieve your goals, but obstacles can be one of the main things that will make you lose focus. One of the key questions you should ask yourself is, "What will stop me making this happen?" This can help to focus your attention on what might get in the way and how you will overcome it.

There are all sorts of reasons why people don't achieve their goals. It could be that they have not planned properly to set themselves up for success from the outset. It could be that they become side-tracked along the way or that they encounter unexpected obstacles. It could be that they simply give up when things get tough. Whatever the reason, if you can identify potential obstacles in advance, you will be in a much better position to overcome them and stay on track to achieving your goal.

Some common obstacles that people can face include:

Lack of time: This is often cited as a major reason why people don't achieve their goals. If you are working full-time, have a young family or other commitments, it can be difficult to find the time to work on your goal. The key is to make time for it. This might mean getting up an hour earlier each day, utilising your lunch break or working for an hour or two in the evening. It might also mean saying 'no' to other commitments in order to make time for your goal.

Lack of money: This can be a major obstacle, especially if you are trying to start your own business. If you don't have the financial resources to get started, it can be difficult to make progress. One way to overcome this is to start small and scale up as your business grows. Another option is to look for sources of funding, such as grants, loans or investment.

Lack of knowledge: If you don't have the necessary skills or knowledge to achieve your goal, it can be difficult to make progress. The key is to identify the gaps in your knowledge and find ways to fill them. This might involve taking a course, reading books, or speaking to experts in your field.

Lack of motivation: It can be difficult to stay motivated when you are working towards a long-term goal. There will be times when you feel like giving up, but it is important to push through and keep going. One way to stay motivated is to break your goal down into smaller, more manageable steps. This will help you to see progress and feel like you are making headway. Another way to stay motivated is to connect with like-minded people who are working towards similar goals. This will give you a support network and help to keep you motivated and on track.

Lack of focus: It is easy to lose focus when you are working towards a goal. This can happen if you become side tracked by other commitments or if you allow yourself to be distracted by things that are not related to your goal. The key is to stay focused and keep your eye on the prize. This might mean setting regular reminders, writing down your goal or speaking to someone who will hold you accountable.

These are just some of the obstacles that people can face when trying to achieve their goals.

When you are aware of potential obstacles, you can create a plan to overcome them. For example, if you know that you are likely to get distracted by social media, then set a timer to limit your time on Facebook or Instagram. Alternatively, you could work in a space that is free from distractions, such as a library or coffee shop. If you know that you are likely to give up when things get tough, then create a support network of friends or family who will encourage you to keep going.

If you can identify the ones that are most likely to impact you, and this is where you have to be brutally honest with yourself, you will be in a better position to overcome them and stay on track.

Do not be the cocky person that I was and say, "Nothing will stop me." Because ultimately it did, and it was stuff that could have easily been prevented. It's not always easy to look at your shortcomings and where you are stopping your own progress, but it's worth it to get to your goal. One of mine was admitting that I really can't work with Netflix playing in the background, even if it's something I've seen a million times. When you know yourself, how you work best and what could stop you, you can create an environment and set up procedures to help you stay focused and on track.

You are not a superwoman (or man) so be prepared. As the saying goes, "Failing to prepare is preparing to fail."

Developing a plan to overcome obstacles that could stop you achieving your goals

So how do you develop a plan to overcome these obstacles? The first step is to identify what these potential roadblocks could be. Once you know what they are, you can then come up with a plan to overcome them.

If you can identify which of these obstacles are most likely to impact your ability to achieve your goals, you can then develop a plan to overcome them. For example, if you know that lack of money is going to be a problem, you can look for ways to raise capital or cut costs. If you know that lack of time is going to be an issue, you can look for ways to streamline your processes or delegate tasks. If you know that fear of failure is going to be a problem, you can look for ways to increase your confidence or reduce the risks involved.

By taking the time to develop a plan to overcome these obstacles, you'll be in a much better position to achieve your goals and grow your business. Your plan will be unique to you and will be dependent upon your obstacles and the skills you can utilise to overcome them.

But remember, obstacles are there to be overcome. Every obstacle is an opportunity to grow and become stronger. The plan you put in place to overcome your obstacles will make you a better entrepreneur and help you achieve even greater things in the future.

Implementing your plan to overcome obstacles that could stop you achieving your goals

Once you have your plan in place, you have to implement it, otherwise you are leaving yourself open to those obstacles stopping your progress.

I'll be honest; most of the plan will probably require you to step outside your comfort zone, but what is worse? Stepping out of your comfort zone or not achieving your goals?

Your comfort zone is a great place, but it's not where the magic happens. The magic is in taking action and putting yourself out there – even if it is scary.

If you want to achieve something different, you have to do something different.

7

THE IMPORTANCE OF CELEBRATING YOUR ACCOMPLISHMENTS

Few people take the time to celebrate their accomplishments. They just move on to the next task, always looking ahead and never taking a moment to enjoy their hard-earned success. But if you want to achieve even more in the future, you need to take the time to celebrate your wins. Here's why:

1) Celebration reinforces your positive behaviour.

When you take the time to celebrate your accomplishments, you're effectively rewarding yourself for a job well done. And just like with any type of reinforcement, this helps to encourage more of the same behaviour in the future. So, if you want to achieve even more, start celebrating your successes along the way.

2) Celebration motivates you to achieve even more.

Reaching a goal is always satisfying, but it can also be motivating. When you see what you're capable of achieving, it gives you the confidence and inspiration to set your sights even higher next time. So, if you want to keep pushing yourself to reach new heights, take the time to celebrate your accomplishments along the way.

3) Celebration helps you enjoy the journey.

The journey to success can be long and challenging, so it's important to enjoy the process as much as the destination. By taking the time to celebrate your accomplishments, you'll find that you appreciate the journey more and feel better about the hard work you're putting in. So, if you want to enjoy the ride, don't forget to celebrate your successes along the way.

4) Celebration builds momentum.

Success begets success, so the more you celebrate your accomplishments, the easier it will be to keep achieving in the future. Just like a snowball rolling down a hill, each success will build on the last, making it easier and easier to achieve even more. So, if you want to create some momentum in your life, start celebrating your accomplishments today.

5) Celebration creates a positive feedback loop.

When you celebrate your accomplishments, you not only reinforce your positive behaviour and motivate yourself to achieve even more, but you also build momentum and create a feedback loop of success. This feedback loop will help you achieve even more in the future, making it easier and easier to reach your goals.

So, if you want to create a cycle of success, start by celebrating your accomplishments.

Celebrating your successes

In order to be successful, it's important to take time to celebrate your accomplishments. This means recognising and acknowledging the hard work you've put in and the progress you've made. It's a way of rewarding yourself and building your confidence. How you celebrate your successes is entirely up to you. It can be something as simple as taking a break to enjoy a cup of coffee or treating yourself to a new outfit, going out for dinner or booking a holiday. Whatever makes you feel good and motivated, do that. Just as your goals are individual to you, the way you celebrate is too. Don't feel you need to celebrate in a certain way just because you've seen someone else do it on social media.

Embarrassing truth time!

I used to think that in order to share my success on social media I had to post a picture of me enjoying a glass of champagne because it's what everyone else seemed to do. The first couple of times, I did go out and buy a bottle of champagne, but a couple of champagne hangovers later I ended up keeping one of the empty bottles of champagne, buying a fancy Veuve Clicquot bottle cover and then whenever I posted that I was celebrating I would pull out the empty bottle wrapped in its jacket and pop a glass next to it filled with....

Appletiser!

Tragic, right? It was something I had seen on a programme called *Make Me an Influencer* or something like that. I cringe now when I think about it.

Now I celebrate how I want, whether that is with a cup of coffee, a fist bump, or blowing my own trumpet. Literally! I have a necklace from Bert Gilbert that makes a noise when you blow it. I wear it when I'm doing a launch and blow it every time I make a sale.

So, my point is, celebrating your success can be done in any way you want to.

Some people like to keep their celebrations low-key while others go all out. There is no right or wrong way to do it. Just make sure you take the time to celebrate your successes, big and small. It will help you stay motivated and focused on your goals.

Just a word of warning. In the same way that there are people around you who didn't get the goals you were setting, there is also a group of people who won't celebrate with you when you achieve them. A lot of it comes from a place of envy. You are showing that it is possible to do something that they perhaps want to achieve but don't want to do the work to make it happen.

Be grateful for the people who are celebrating you and don't let a few negative Nancies hold you back from shouting out loud about your achievements.

Setting new goals after reaching old ones

Once you have celebrated the success of achieving your goal, it's time to set a new one. A goal is only the beginning of the journey. Once you reach that goal, it's time to set a new one. Otherwise, you'll find yourself at a standstill. Goal setting is important because it gives you something to strive for. It challenges you to keep growing and keeps you motivated. When you achieve a goal, don't be content to stay where you are. Set your sights even higher and keep pushing yourself. There are no limits to what you can achieve if you set your mind to it.

Maybe you want to achieve something even bigger and better this time around. Or maybe you want to set a new goal in a different area of your life. Either way, goal setting is an important part of continued success.

It is important to define your new goal clearly. Just as you did with your previous goal, take some time to think about what you want to accomplish. What is your endgame? What steps will you need to take to get there? When you set new goals, you use the same process as you did with your original goal. You start by thinking about what you want to achieve and then develop a plan to make it happen.

Your previous successes can give you the confidence you need to take on even bigger challenges. Having achieved your previous goals, you have a much better knowledge of what you are capable of achieving. When you set a new goal, keep this in mind. If you have achieved something great before, you can achieve it again so don't be afraid to dream big.

By setting new goals after reaching old ones, you can stay motivated, focused and continue making progress.

The importance of taking time for yourself

It is important to take time for yourself after accomplishing something great. This enables you to reflect on your success and allows you to enjoy it. It also gives you the opportunity to plan your next move and prepare yourself for future challenges.

As busy entrepreneurs we are often on a treadmill, quickly moving on to the next thing. We give a fleeting acknowledgment to what we have achieved and then on we go. This can work for a while, but it's not sustainable in the long term.

It is essential to our well-being, both physically and mentally, to take time to celebrate our successes. This could be something as small as taking a few minutes at the end of each day to reflect on what went well or it could be something more significant, like taking a day off after hitting an important milestone.

The benefits of taking time to celebrate our accomplishments are numerous. It can help us to:

- Reflect on our successes and learn from them
- Enjoy our achievements instead of just rushing on to the next thing
- Build our confidence and self-belief
- Stay motivated and focused
- Prepare ourselves mentally and emotionally for future challenges

Not only does this allow us to enjoy our success, but it also gives us the opportunity to learn from our achievements. When we take the time to celebrate, we are able to step back and reflect on what worked well and what could be improved upon. This information is invaluable as we move forward and continue to strive for success.

Using celebration to achieve success

If you want to achieve success, you need to set your sights high and celebrate your accomplishments along the way. That's because celebration is a powerful tool for achieving goals. When you take the time to celebrate your successes, big and small, you're sending a message to yourself that you're on the right track. This in turn helps to motivate and inspire you to keep going, even when the going gets tough. So don't be afraid to set your sights high and celebrate your accomplishments along the way. It just might be the key to achieving your biggest goals.

8

GOAL SETTING FOR DIFFERENT AREAS OF YOUR LIFE

Most people think about goal setting in terms of their professional lives. But what about your personal life? Or your health and wellbeing? If you want to achieve success in all areas of your life, you need to set goals for each of them.

Without specific goals to strive for, it's easy to become bogged down in the day-to-day and lose sight of what you're working towards. However, goal setting is not a one-size-fits-all endeavour. The goals you set for your professional life may be very different from the goals you set for your personal life. For example, you may have a goal to advance to a leadership position at work, while your goal for your personal life may be to spend more time with your family. The important thing is to take the time to consider thoughtfully what you want to achieve in each area of your life and create specific goals that will help you get there. By taking the time to set realistic and achievable goals, you'll be putting yourself on the path to success in all areas of your life.

Setting goals for your personal life

Action without a goal is like sailing without an end destination. You may be going somewhere, but you will never reach your potential or realise your dreams. This is why goal setting is so important in every area of our lives, including our personal lives. By setting personal goals, we give ourselves a road map to success and a way to measure our progress along the way.

In a recent study[1] it was found that when people set goals for themselves, they were more likely to achieve them if those objectives had some relationship with an unmet need or desire.

Have a think about your personal life. Is there anything you would like to change? Anything you would like to achieve? Something that has perhaps been on your bucket list for ages? You know, the one where you say, "I've always wanted to do that." Do it!

If you're not sure where to start, here are some examples of personal goals you can set for yourself:

- Spend less money
- Save more money
- Get out of debt
- Get a degree
- Learn a new skill
- Master a new hobby
- Volunteer more
- Spend more time with family and friends
- Travel more
- Take up a new sport or activity

No matter what goals you set for yourself, don't try and do them all at once. People fail so often with New Year's resolutions because they try to implement too many habits at the same time. Trying to accomplish too much at once can be overwhelming and lead to discouragement. Start small and build up from there.

I linked some of my goals to charity. When I jumped out of a plane and walked on fire, I used them as an opportunity to raise money for a charity close to my heart. It makes me feel like I am making a difference, not just in my life but in the lives of others too. When it comes to personal goals, we can sometimes feel guilty for doing stuff for ourselves. If we can help others at the same time, it's a win-win!

Setting goals for your professional life

Most of the goals we set 'professionally' are for our business, but we can also set professional goals for ourselves as individuals. Set goals for yourself professionally to help improve your development and this in turn will help your business to thrive.

Some examples of professional goals are:

- Develop a personal brand
- Create a strong online presence
- Build a supportive network of like-minded individuals
- Engage in continuous learning opportunities
- Attend industry events and conferences
- Take an online course
- Get better at time management

Your professional goals can be short-term and tactical to help you today, this month, or this year and they can also be more strategic, long-term goals that will help you in the next few years. Choose what works for you. Don't be afraid to mix it up.

Setting goals for your health and wellbeing

When you get on an aeroplane and watch the safety demonstration, the hostess will always say, "Put your own oxygen mask on first before helping others." This is true in every area of life. If you don't take care of yourself, you won't be able to take care of anything or anyone else. So, one of your goals should be to focus on your own health and wellbeing. That means your mental wellbeing as well as your physical wellbeing. When you're feeling good physically and mentally, it's easier to stay motivated and focused on your goals.

Here are some ideas for setting goals for health and wellbeing:

- Physical wellbeing: I will exercise for thirty minutes, three times a week.
- Mental wellbeing: I will meditate for ten minutes every day.
- Emotional wellbeing: I will journal for fifteen minutes every evening.
- Spiritual wellbeing: I will read one chapter of a self-help book every week.

Living with bipolar, I know from experience the importance of health and wellness goals. I had a mental breakdown in 2012 and was diagnosed with bipolar. I was put on anti-depressants and for a long time I took them religiously and expected them to solve everything. But I learned that they were only half of the journey. I had to put in the work too. What did I expect the tablets to do if nothing else was changing? It would be like papering over a crack in the wall. The crack would still be there. So, while I still take my 'happy pills', I also set health and wellness goals and mentally I'm in the best place I've been in years. (The health goals are still pending – I enjoy Krispy Kreme donuts too much.)

Of course, you can tailor these goals to suit your own needs and preferences. The important thing is that you make time for yourself and invest in your own health and happiness. By doing so, you'll be much better equipped to deal with the challenges and stresses of daily life – and to reach your personal and professional goals too.

Using goal setting to achieve success in all areas of your life

Setting goals in all areas of your life is a crucial step on the road to success. All the different goals you set will have an effect on each other when you achieve them. They are all interlinked. And that's why setting goals in different areas of your life is so important.

Your career, your personal life, your health, your relation-ships… all these areas are important, and when you're striving for success in one area, the other areas will be affected too. So, it's important to set goals in each of these areas, and to make sure that they're all working together towards your overall success.

9

THE POWER OF SETTING LONG-TERM GOALS

L ong-term goals give you a sense of purpose and something to strive for even when the going gets tough, but some people seem to have a phobia of setting long-term goals. They are ok with short goals, but long-term goals make them super uncomfortable. I've been working with a client who really struggled with setting longer term goals. She was great in the short term but she just couldn't do anything over ¬six to twelve months. This is a problem because in order to grow your business, you need to be able to set long-term goals and stay focused on them.

In the first few years of your business, it's easy to get caught up in the day-to-day grind and lose sight of the bigger picture. This is especially true for entrepreneurs, who often have a lot of competing demands on their time. Setting long-term goals can help you stay focused on what's important and ensure that your business is moving in the right direction.

Short-term goals are important, but they should always be in service of your long-term goals. For example, if your goal is to grow your business by 20% this year, you'll need to set some shorter term goals that will help you achieve that. But if all you're focused on are short-term goals, you may not end up where you want to be in the long run.

It can be helpful to think of your long-term goals as your North Star. They should be something that you can always come back to when you're feeling lost or uncertain.

Brainstorming long-term goals

The best way to achieve success in your business is to set long-term goals. This means that you need to take the time to think about where you see your business in the future, and what you need to do to get there. Long-term goals give you a roadmap for your business and help ensure that you are moving in the right direction.

Setting long-term goals can be difficult, especially if you are just starting out in business. However, it is essential to have a clear idea of where you want your business to go. Without long-term goals, it will be very difficult to achieve lasting success.

When I started my first business, I never had any long-term goals. To be fair, I never had any goals. I sort of fell into my business. Let me explain.

My first business was a cake business. I was a cake maker. I didn't set out in life to become a cake maker. In fact, I had a career as a supervisor in a foreign exchange. Then I had kids, which meant my career went from full-time, to part-time, to no time.

Part of being a full-time mum meant that I made cakes for my daughters' birthdays. For a bit of context, my nan made cakes, my mum made birthday cakes for me and my sisters, and so I inherited that gene. It turned out I was pretty good at it, and so I got asked by their playmates' mums to make cakes for their children and it grew from there. The business just happened. No business plans. No goals.

But, as I touched on earlier in the book, having no goals and no sense of direction meant the business took on a mind of its own and led to my breakdown. While it may seem odd to say, I was grateful for that breakdown and the questions that arose from it as I was able to take a step back and ask, *What do I want?* I didn't want to give up the business. It gave me an identity other than being someone's mum and wife. But it clearly couldn't continue as it was. And that was the point that I set long-term goals.

I took the time to sit down and decide what I really wanted this business to achieve; what I wanted my business to look like in five years' time. And this is what brainstorming long-term goals is all about. It's about taking the time to think about where you want your business to go, and what you need to do to get there.

Some questions you could ask yourself during this process include:

- What do I want my business to achieve in the next five years?
- What do I want my business to look like in five years' time?
- What do I want my life to look like in five years' time?

- What products or services do I want to be offering in five years' time?
- What do I need to do to make my business a success?
- What are my long-term goals for my business?

If five years seems too scary, start with two years. But the important thing is to start thinking about the future of your business and what you want to achieve. Only then can you start putting together a plan to make it happen.

Setting SMART long-term goals

In order to set effective long-term goals, they need to be SMART: Specific, Measurable, Achievable, Relevant, and Time-bound.

For example, a goal of 'growing your business' is too vague and lacks specificity. A better goal would be 'to increase sales by 20% by the end of the year.' This goal is specific, measurable, achievable, relevant, and time-bound.

The more specific you can be about your goals the better.

That being said, don't get so caught up in the details that you never set long-term goals. A lot of the specifics of long-term goals do change over time anyway. Look at the Covid pandemic for example – that threw a lot of people's plans out the window (including my own) and a lot of people had to pivot and divert. *But* because they had the long-term goals in place in the first place, they were in a much better position to do so.

So, if you haven't already, sit down and think about what your long-term goals are for your business. Once you have them, break them down into smaller, more manageable chunks so that you can start taking steps.

The main thing is to have a clear idea of the overall direction you want your business to go in the long run.

At all times when you are setting those longer term goals, keep asking yourself *why?* Why are you setting this goal? Why is it important to you? What will achieving this goal allow you to do?

If you can keep those questions at the forefront of your mind, you'll be more likely to set goals that you are in alignment with.

Mapping out a plan to achieve your long-term goals

After you have brainstormed your long-term goals, it is important to start working towards them. This means setting short-term goals that will help you achieve your long-term goals. Without actionable steps, your long-term goals will remain nothing more than a dream.

Start by taking some time to think about what you need to do in the next twelve months to begin working towards your long-term goals. Then, break these down into smaller goals that you can achieve each month. For example, if one of your long-term goals is to double your income in the next year, smaller goals for this could be to increase sales by 10% each month or to launch a new product each quarter. Those small goals all go towards the achievement of the longer term goal.

If you find yourself getting stuck, ask yourself these questions:

- What is my end goal?
- What are some milestones I can hit along the way?
- What specific steps do I need to take to achieve my goal?
- How can I measure my progress?
- By when do I want to achieve this goal?

Answering these questions will help you create specific, achievable, relevant goals that you can hit. And once you start hitting your short-term goals, you'll be well on your way to achieving your long-term goals.

Using long-term goal setting to achieve success

If you are struggling with setting long-term goals, here are a few tips to help you get started:

1. Take some time out for yourself. This may seem like an obvious one, but it is so important. In order to be able to set long-term goals, you need to have a clear head. This means taking some time out for yourself, away from your business. Whether it's going for a walk, reading a book, or just sitting in silence, you need to give yourself time to think.
2. Write down your goals. This may seem like a no-brainer, but it is so important to write down your goals. Having them written down will help to make them more real and ensure that you are more likely to stick to them.

3. Set realistic goals. It is important to set goals that are achievable. There is no point in setting a goal that is impossible to achieve, as you will only end up feeling discouraged. Set goals that challenge you but that are still achievable.

4. Make a plan. Once you have set your goals, it is important to make a plan of how you are going to achieve them. This will ensure that you are taking the necessary steps to reach your goals and help to keep you on track.

5. Get some accountability. One of the best ways to ensure that you stick to your goals is to get some accountability. This could be in the form of a business coach or mentor, or even just a friend or family member with whom you check in.

And remember, it's never too late to set a long-term goal. My business was six years old before I took time to reflect on what I wanted it to look like in the future. If you don't have one right now, sit down and take some time to think about where you want your business to be in five years or ten years. Then start working backwards to create a plan for how you're going to get there. Just don't get so caught up in the long-term goal that you forget to work on the short-term goals needed to make it happen.

10

HOW TO CREATE A GOAL-SETTING PLAN

You have set your goals. You've made sure they are smart. Now what? How do you turn your goals into a plan that will help you achieve them?

Creating a goal-setting plan is not difficult, but it does require some careful thought and attention to detail. By taking the time to create a well thought out goal-setting plan, you increase your chances of achieving your goals significantly.

Here are some tips on how to create a goal-setting plan:

1. Write down your goals.

This may seem like a no-brainer, but it's important to put your goals in writing. Seeing them in black and white will help you to focus on them and keep them at the forefront of your mind. You need to have each and every goal that you want to achieve written down: the business goals; the personal goals; the learning goals. All of them.

2. Make a list of action items.

Once you have your goals written down, it's time to start thinking about how you're going to achieve them. What steps do you need to take in order to reach your goal? Make a list of these action items and be as specific as possible.

You have to do this for every single goal.

For example:

A goal of mine (at the time of writing) is to grow my YouTube channel. Why? Because growing my channel will help me to reach more people, which will enable me to help more people move forward and grow their businesses. It goes with my values that knowledge should be accessible.

In terms of it being a smart goal, I want to reach 1000 subscribers and get 4,000 hours of views. Why? Because that's when I can apply for monetisation and generate a passive income from my channel.

So, what action steps will I take to make this happen?

- Create a content calendar with a focus on valuable and engaging content that my audience needs.
- Record my podcast as video to use as content.
- Constantly listen to what my audience is asking. Listen to what they need help with and make videos to solve their pain points.
- Shoot and edit videos regularly – a minimum of one per week. Repurpose videos from other social media platforms such as Facebook lives.
- Optimise my videos for YouTube SEO.

- Promote my videos through social media and other channels. Schedule weekly posts that lead to my YouTube channel. If someone asks a question and I have a YouTube video with the answer, direct them to my channel with a link if possible.
- Engage with my audience regularly and reply to comments.
- Analyse my analytics to see what's working and adjust my strategy accordingly.

I do this step for each and every goal. If my goal is an experience, for example, a holiday or a trip to the theatre, I put a monetary value of how much it will cost. I can then know how much I need to earn to make those goals happen and I turn that into a money goal. I need to earn x amount of money. How am I going to do it? What do I need to do? What do I need to sell to make that happen?

For every goal I have at least five pieces of action that I am going to take to make it happen.

3. Create a timeline.

In order for your goal-setting plan to be effective, you need to create a timeline for yourself. When do you want to achieve your goal? What's the deadline? What milestones do you want to hit along the way? By creating a timeline, you'll have a better sense of what needs to be done and when.

When setting deadlines, make sure they are realistic. There's no point in setting a deadline of one week to achieve a goal that will realistically take six months.

I do a big goal-setting session at the end of each year ready for the year ahead. What do I want to achieve the following year? How will I do it? What goals will I achieve when?

I map out the year ahead and I can then break that down into quarterly, then monthly and then weekly goals. Those bite-sized chunks are always so much easier. That YouTube goal of 1000 subscribers is only an average of twenty per week when broken down.

When it comes to my money goal for the year, I work out what I need to do to earn it – what I need to sell. I write down all my products, offerings and services and how much they cost. I can then work out how many of each I need to sell over the course of the year to achieve that money goal.

I then map out exactly what I am going to sell *and* when.

I do this on an A2 piece of paper. I fold it into twelve and I write a month at the top of each section. In each month I write down what I'm going to be selling – my main offering for each month, whether that is my course, or opening the doors to my membership, or being an affiliate for someone else's product. Knowing what I am selling and when is why I am able to achieve results, because for every product or service there is a plan of action for how I will sell it.

Of course, this isn't set in stone. Other things may come along which mean you have to move stuff around. When I did my first affiliate launch for someone, that wasn't in my original plan. Doing this isn't about it being set in stone but about being able to make educated decisions based on the strategy you have planned. You may add in an extra product, for example. That's ok.

When doing your timeline, make sure you add key dates if your products and services are affected by them. Perhaps you launch certain things at certain times. If you are considering doing Black Friday, think about it sooner rather than later. Again, be proactive with what you are planning to sell.

4. Time block the action

You have created a timeline. You know the action steps. Now time block the action into the diary to make it happen.

I time block my action steps into the diary. I have at least one day dedicated to working *on* my business and taking action towards achieving those goals. Whatever actions need to be done to make my goals happen, I time block them in. And when it's time blocked in my diary – I stick to it!

5. Set reminders.

One of the best ways to make sure you stick to your goal-setting plan is to set reminders for yourself. Whether it's a daily email reminder or a weekly meeting with yourself to review your progress, setting reminders will help you stay on track.

Each week, as I time block the week ahead, I take time to review what I achieved the previous week. Did I hit my weekly goals? If not, why not? What changes can I make to ensure that I hit the goal I set myself for that month? (Remember, your weekly goals are there so you achieve your monthly goal.)

I do the same at the end of each month. I look at each goal. Am I on track? Am I where I need to be at this point in time? Yes? Great, I'll keep doing what I'm doing. No? I'll review what I am doing and make changes. Things will come up that you didn't plan for. You may need to make adjustments to your plan along the way. That's ok. The important thing is that you review your progress regularly and make changes as needed.

By doing this every week and every month, it means that you aren't wasting your time taking action that doesn't work. You're only doing what does. And by making those changes you are one step closer to achieving your goal.

6. Get accountability partners.

In addition to setting reminders for yourself, another great way to stay on track is to get accountability partners. These are people whom you check in with on a regular basis to update them on your progress. Having someone to be accountable to will help you stay focused and motivated.

7. Take action!

The final and most important step in the goal-setting process is to take action. Without taking action, none of the other steps matter. Your goal-setting plan is worthless if you don't follow through and take action.

Creating a goal-setting plan is an important step in the goal-setting process. By taking the time to create a well thought out plan, you increase your chances of achieving your goals significantly. Implementing your goal-setting plan is just as important. Don't create a pretty plan just so it looks nice on your wall. Take action towards achieving your goals.

11

FINAL TIPS FOR STAYING FOCUSED AND ORGANISED

When it comes to achieving your goals, staying focused and organised is essential. Without these two key ingredients, it will be difficult to make progress. However, if you can focus your efforts and stay organised, you will be well on your way to success.

This final chapter provides helpful tips on how to stay on track and make the most of your time. Whether you are just starting out or have been in business for a few years, this chapter will give you the tools and advice you need to succeed. Some of these we have covered in more detail in previous chapters, but it is always useful to be reminded.

Create a goal-setting plan

One of the best ways to stay focused and organised when working towards your goals is to create a goal-setting plan. This plan should include what your goals are, how you will achieve them, and when you want to achieve them by. Having a plan will help to keep you focused and on track. If you find yourself deviating from the plan, take a step back and reassess your goals to see if they are still realistic.

Break your goals down into manageable tasks

If your goals seem overwhelming, break them down into smaller, more manageable tasks. This will make it easier to complete each task and keep track of your progress. Make sure to set a deadline for each task so you can stay on track.

Set a deadline for each task

Giving yourself a deadline for each task will help you stay focused and on track. Make sure to determine when a goal should be accomplished. This will ensure it is done in a timely fashion and does not become an overwhelming project. People procrastinate when a goal seems daunting and without a set timeframe: it is easy to keep pushing it back. Attach a date to each goal so it becomes a priority and work can begin immediately. Change the deadline if necessary but always have one in place. Doing so will increase the likelihood of goal achievement instead of remaining another unfulfilled dream.

Time block your week

Another great way to stay focused and organised when working towards your goals is to time block your week. This means setting aside certain times for certain tasks related to your goals. For example, you may want to set aside Monday mornings from 9am to10am to work on goal planning. Having a schedule like this will help to keep you focused and on track.

Make use of technology

There are various pieces of technology that can help you stay focused and organised when working towards your goals. For example, you can use a goal-setting app to help you track your progress and keep on track. You can also use a calendar app to schedule in time for goal-related tasks. Utilising technology in this way can be a great help in staying focused and organised.

Set reminders

Another helpful tip for staying focused and organised when working towards your goals is to set reminders. You can set reminders on your phone, in your calendar, or even write them down on a piece of paper. Having regular reminders will help to keep you on track and ensure that you don't forget about your goals.

Talk to someone

Do not be afraid to ask for help. There is no shame in admitting that you need assistance. Asking for help can be the difference between reaching your goal and giving up altogether. If you're struggling to stay focused and organised when working towards your goals, it may be helpful to talk to someone about it. Talking to someone can help to give you some accountability and may also provide some helpful tips.

Get a planner

If you're struggling with staying organised, it may be helpful to get a planner. This can be an electronic or physical planner.

Having a place to write down your goals, tasks and progress can be very helpful in keeping you on track. I have many goal-setting planners available to purchase on Amazon.

Take breaks

It is important to remember that you can't work on your goals all the time. Working towards a goal can be taxing, both mentally and physically. It's important to take breaks and allow yourself some time to relax. Taking breaks can help to prevent burnout and will also give you some time to refocus. It does not mean you are slacking off; it just means you are taking care of yourself so you can be more productive in the long run.

Working towards your goals can be a challenge, but it's important to stay focused and organised. By following these tips, you can help to ensure that you stay on track and achieve your goals.

Reward yourself for completing tasks

After you complete a task, give yourself a small reward. This can help motivate you to keep going and reach your goal. The rewards should be commensurate with the difficulty of the task; for example, if you completed a difficult task, give yourself a bigger reward than if you completed an easy task.

Keep a positive attitude

It is important to maintain a positive attitude when working towards a goal. Having a positive outlook will help you stay motivated and focused on your goals. If you find yourself getting discouraged, take a step back and remind yourself why you are working towards the goal in the first place.

Persevere when things get tough

There will be times when it seems like you are never going to reach your goal. During these times, it is important to persevere and keep working towards your goal. Remember why you started working towards the goal in the first place and use that as motivation to keep going.

By implementing everything that you have learned from this book, you will go from goal setter to goal getter in no time. Remember to take things one step at a time, stay focused and organised, and most importantly, don't give up. With perseverance and hard work, you can achieve anything you set your mind to. *You* are the one in control of achieving your goals and living the life you want to live!

A PARTING ANECDOTE

"Dad – I can't get out of Cambridge," I cried down the phone.

"What do you mean, you can't get out of Cambridge?" he replied.

"I came in for a meeting and every road I take to leave brings me back in," I wailed.

"What do you want me to do?"

"Come and find me and guide me out...."

This is the true story of a telephone conversation I had with my poor dad back in 1997 BSN (Before Sat Nav). I was working for McDonalds, and I had been promoted to area training coordinator, so I got to travel to stores across Herts, Beds, Bucks and Cambridge to improve their training systems and record keeping.

On this one occasion I had been sent to a store in Cambridge. It was a great day, and it was time for me to head home. But these were the pre sat nav days. I couldn't just pop a postcode into my phone and get directed home by a firm (and sometimes passive-aggressive) voice.

Because my dad was an area sales manager before he retired, he travelled around the country a lot and always seemed to know exactly where he was going every time he sat behind the wheel of his car. Wherever we had to go, whenever we had to go, he got us there. So, me being me, figuring I had the same genes as Daddy, this naïve nineteen-year-old headed into Cambridge full of self-confidence and a clear side order of delusion.

What I didn't know at that point was that before every trip my dad made, he would spend time planning the route with a high-lighter pen and one of those large paper maps. (Remember them? Once you had opened them they took up the entire front of the car and you could never fold them up the same way. It was like a travel origami challenge.)

I had seen the pile of maps in his office. But because I hadn't ever seen the preparation my dad had done in advance behind the scenes, I just headed out on a wing and a prayer, hoping that I would succeed, but in reality not being at all prepared for it. Because I had always thought it worked for him, I just assumed it would work for me.

But every road I tried to take out of Cambridge somehow took me right back to the same place and that was not where I wanted to be. I just wanted to go home but I was stuck on this damn ring road, moving forward but never to the right place and the day was getting later and later.

I see so many people doing the same in business. They are moving, but not in the right direction. Getting stuck at roadblocks and not knowing how to get past. They try to follow other people's road maps and have no idea where they might even end up or how long the journey will take so they aren't prepared and run out of petrol before they have even got started.

So many people start a business with no idea of where they want to go or what they want the business to achieve.

The idea that people just get behind the wheel of a car and head off to a destination unknown belongs in movies and TV shows. Do you know anyone in real life who has ever woken up one morning and just jumped in the car, turned the key in the ignition and driven off, seeing where the roads take them and where they end up?

Of course not.

Before we start any road trip, we know the end destination. We know where we are headed. We make sure we have a full tank of petrol. We have snacks for the duration. And nowadays, with sat nav so readily available in vehicles and on phones, you wouldn't dream of setting off to a destination you have never been before without popping in the postcode. That reassuring, yet somewhat passive-aggressive, voice is there to instruct you on every step of the journey. *"At the next roundabout take the third exit."*

We can even check beforehand how long the journey will take so we know what time we need to leave and thanks to the joys of technology, journey duration estimations take into account traffic at any given time. It's amazing.

Of course, sat navs have their off days. They tell you to turn right when there is no right turning. Or, more annoyingly, they say you have reached your destination and actually it's still a mile down the road. But for the most part, they are pretty reliable.

Setting goals for your business is what a postcode is to a sat nav. You have to programme in the destination. You need to have a predetermined idea of what you want to achieve and where you want to end up, else you may end up heading in the wrong direction, miles out of your way, doing something that you don't want to do.

You don't want your business to be some sort of magical mystery tour. They don't work. Even the Beatles' *Magical Mystery Tour* was a flop.

In fact, what turned into a bigger event than the Beatles filming *Magical Mystery Tour* was the entourage that began to surround the bus, wondering what the 'tour' was all about. People followed the bus for miles and caused traffic jams. People who saw the bus go by expected an event of some kind, but none had been planned. In trying to be spontaneous, nobody had worked out a destination for the bus or the trip. All this fuss for no end destination.

If the Beatles can't make it work, we have no hope.

There are many times in life we can be spontaneous. But running a business is not that time. Goals need to be set. Destinations need to be planned.

Ideally this would all be in place before you start your business, but it's never too late to programme your sat nav. I'd been running my business for years before I finally entered the destination. I finally had a clear vision of what I wanted to achieve and what I wanted to accomplish and after I programmed my own sat nav I got there a whole lot quicker.

It is time to put your own personal road map in place for setting, planning and achieving your goals. Whether they are business or personal goals, having a road map in place will get you to where you want to be. What's the overall destination? What stops do you want or need to make along the way? Create the route that will take you to your overall goal, avoiding any road humps, traffic jams and road closures.

And just like your car on a long road trip needs a regular service to keep it performing efficiently, your road map will need regular reviews too. Perhaps since starting out, a road-block you need to avoid has popped up so you need to put a diversion in place and reroute. Perhaps you need to add another stop on the way to that final destination.

And remember that your road map to achieving your goals will be different to that of other people. They are heading to a different destination. Your journey could be in a completely opposite direction. Your journey may take a little bit longer. You may have more, or indeed fewer, pit stops.

And watch out for those pesky passengers in the back seat. You know, the ones who can't drive but think they know best. You don't want to end up heading in the wrong direction because back seat Bess piped up and convinced you it was a great idea to come off a junction early.

The perfect road trip takes time to plan. So does setting goals. But the journey is always a lot less bumpy with a little preparation. And that's not to say there won't be bumps in the road, but you will be a lot more prepared to drive at them head on with the right preparation in place. At least you know where you are going.

And as much as the destination is the end goal, it is important to enjoy the journey along the way.

My dad never did come to get me. He got out his trusty maps at home, figured out where I was, and gave me the road numbers I needed to get me home. If only I had done this in the first place, I would have got where I wanted to be so much quicker.

ABOUT THE AUTHOR
SHELLY SHULMAN

Shelly Shulman is a goal setting and accountability coach. She has sixteen years of business experience with award-winning success. She helps business owners and entrepreneurs grow their businesses with practical support and advice so that they can move forward with their business and get the results they crave.

Shelly is a self-proclaimed organisational wizard: setting goals, making plans and putting strategy in place is what has enabled her to grow her business. This Bedfordshire-based powerhouse helps people achieve their goals by providing insightful coaching, sensible advice, and ongoing support.

 instagram.com/theshellyshulman

KIND WORDS

Thanks for a great session, Shelly! It gave me the encouragement and confidence to walk away and plan to implement goals that I have been putting off for a while. It was great to really break my plans down into bite-sized, manageable tasks and finally put them into a plan of action. This session made me understand how to tackle my overwhelm and make progress in small steps.

PRITI KAUR JENKINS - TYLDESLEY CAKES

———

Before my session with Shelly, I was feeling a little anxious and confused about the direction I wanted to take part of my business. I seemed to have lots of questions but not much clarity when trying to find the answers. Since speaking with Shelly, I have had a series of revelations and, subsequently, have been able to action new ideas and objectives in my work. I really appreciate how down to earth Shelly is and how comfortable she made me feel. Although our sessions are always professional and informative, I always feel like I'm just chatting to a friend! Thank you, Shelly for being so helpful and supportive; your advice and support has been a huge help for both me and my business!

ANNIE CUTTS – ANNIE ELIZABETH CAKE
DESIGN

———

Before I worked with Shelly, I had no idea what a strategy was! I was just winging it day by day and feeling so lost. I had no direction. I had no idea how to plan ahead or even know what I could offer as a lead magnet. Once we got talking, it became apparent I actually do have lots of ideas that I could use as a lead magnet. Shelly explained how I could use them and when to do them. This was a massive breakthrough because I just didn't know what I could offer. Since our time together I have mapped out next year and it seems achievable – it feels like a weight has lifted. I see now how important a strategy is to have. I have something to work towards now!

HELEN KELYNACK – SENARA'S SISTER
HYPNOTHERAPY

————

I took part in Shelly's Plan-a-polooza - which was basically a free festival full of lots of learnings, business support & fun!

This helped me learn new business tips and also how to do certain things, like why to have a private FB group - which I did immediately after the session. It also made me aware of lots of other entrepreneurs/pages to follow that have been when I am now and fills me with the hope that I can do it too!

Since then I've followed Shelly and as if by magic she also became my OTM pod lead (number 1 of course) when I bit the bullet to invest in myself in March 2022.

In the pod she is such a support to us all, always helping, checking in, cannot do enough to motivate us, shares her knowledge & I'm sure we've all signed up to her super useful you tube tutorials - that are so easy to follow!

Anyway in short, I'm glad our paths crossed & I know she'll be in my life now

SARAH BRAEBAUM – THE GINGHAM FLAMINGO

————

I love Shelly's easy to follow videos from how to set up your Facebook page to optimising your bio. I have set a date to follow a video a day once I'm back from holiday and implement what I've learnt before going on to the next video! It's my focus for this Summer!

I bought the business boost pack a few months ago and have had great success in building my Instagram page and increasing my reach and engagement so I can't wait to follow her advice for my Facebook group and page.

I highly recommend any entrepreneur to follow Shelly! You'll learn something new everyday!

MANGLA SACHDEV – BUSINESS IN A BAG

———

I own, mange and work in three businesses and decided in an attempt to stop trading my time for money, I would start a digital business involving business courses, a membership and subscription box. My biggest problem is my butterfly brain and I would constantly start off in the office in the morning and flutter my way through a dozen completely different tasks at the same time then wonder exactly what it was I'm supposed to be doing!! Getting to the end of the week and realising I'd not done some things but had done others that could have waited... Constantly feeling like I'd not actually achieved anything as I still had overdue 'jobs'

That was before I found Shelly's time blocking and goal setting. I now spend half an hour on a Monday morning looking at my 'to do' list and I block the week into fixed appointments then section the rest of the time into projects from the list, including setting time for checking emails and notifications. My time is sorted and the goals are set. When I reach the end of the week I can now see that I've ticked projects off my list and achieved my short term goals.

EMMA GREENEP – EG BUSINESS SOLUTIONS

———

REFERENCES

8. Goal Setting for Different Areas of your Life

1. Beyond Self-Actualization – Greene and Burke 2007

Printed in Great Britain
by Amazon

85811508R00061